BLUE SPRUCE
KIWANIS
EVERGREEN, COLORADO

# Mountain Neighbors
# Cookie Cookbook

*Published by*
**Pinecone Book Company**
BethFosterED@gmail.com

# Table of Contents

# IMPORTANT
## *Read Before Baking!*

**ALWAYS read through the recipe before you start.** This the Golden Rule when it comes to baking. It's imperative to read a recipe through before even thinking about starting. Ideally, you should read through it twice. You'll get an idea for what you'll need to do and when exactly you'll need to do it. Plus, you don't want to get a third of the way through making the recipe only to find out that your cookie dough needs to be chilled overnight. **(We've put chilling instructions in bold type so you'll spot them quickly.)**

**ALWAYS preheat the oven fully before baking.** It is imperative that you preheat the oven, as putting baked goods into a not-hot-enough oven can result in a less than ideal outcome. Make sure your oven gets to temperature before you put your masterpiece in there! We found that using an oven thermometer is a good idea; it's rare that an oven is exactly calibrated. Oven temperatures are posted in bold type near the end of each recipe.

**ALWAYS bake a test batch before continuing with the recipe,** and let your test cookies cool completely before making any adjustments. This allows you to: **1)** Get the texture just right—cakey, crispy, chewy. **2)** Right-size your cookies. **3)** Make sure your oven temperature is accurate. **4)** Check that your ingredients are still fresh. (You'll be able to taste it if they're not.) **5)** If you're trying a new recipe, make sure you actually like it. **6)** Freeze a batch for later. **7)** Eat some cookies now, of course!

**A few important recipe notes ...**

- Brown sugar should always be packed.
- Spices are ground unless otherwise noted.
- Flour is all-purpose unless otherwise noted.

**More notes are included in the "Cookie Wisdom" feature throughout the book.**

# Introduction

**WELCOME to the *Blue Spruce Kiwanis Mountain Neighbors Cookie Cookbook.*** We thrilled you're here, and we know you're going to find many recipes that become traditions in your family. We tested these recipes, so we know what we're talking about!

**These recipes are tested for high altitude.** One of our test kitchens was in Evergreen (about 7,200') and one was in Bailey (8,600'). But this doesn't mean every recipe will work perfectly for you—it's vitally important that you bake a test batch before proceeding with the to allow you to make adjustments as needed (see previous page).

A huge thank-you goes out to the 43 contributors who shared, in total, 66 of their favorite recipes. Our cookie bakers all live or work (or both) in our mountain community, hailing from Evegreen, Kittredge, Conifer, Bailey, Genesee. Idaho Springs, and as far away as Grand Lake.

Another big thank-you to the Cookbook Team, who gathered and tested recipes and shared their amazing cookie knowledge to make this book useful to bakers of all levels, from beginner to expert. Members of the team are: **Beth Foster, Debbie Schwartz, Jill Garrou, Judy Tersteeg,** and **Kristy Tolan**.

Thank you to Beth Foster Editorial & Design and Pinecone Book Company for donating their services to design, build, and publish the cookbook. Thanks to Beth and Debbie Schwartz for the hours they spent proofreading the book; if readers find any errors, Beth and Debbie apologize profusely and hope they weren't major ones.

And special thanks to Blue Spruce Kiwanis, for sponsoring the cookbook and covering the cost of printing. They will donate all proceeds from the sale of this book to food banks in our community.

**Now ... ready, *set*, GO! Happy baking!**

*Dedicated to the memory of Susan Stearns and Lee Sweetland, who both loved cookies.*

# Oatmeal Chocolate Chip Cookies

*I have made these for years and, when I met Bjorn, I made them for his relatives in Sweden. Cookies weren't a thing there in the '90s, so I had difficulty finding brown sugar. His family loved them. They also don't drink flavored coffee in Sweden, so I brought Vanilla Nut coffee from the U.S. to go with the cookies!*

**MAKES 5–6 DOZEN**

1 cup butter at room temperature
1 cup brown sugar
1 cup granulated sugar
3 eggs
1 teaspoon vanilla
2½ cups flour
1 teaspoon salt
1 teaspoon cinnamon
2 teaspoons baking soda
2 cups oatmeal
1 12-oz. package chocolate chips
¾ cup chopped nuts

Cream together butter and sugars. Add eggs and vanilla and mix well. Add flour, salt, cinnamon and baking soda to butter mixture, mix well. Stir in oatmeal, chocolate chips and nuts. Dough will be stiff.

Drop by heaping teaspoons onto ungreased cookie sheet or roll into small balls and flatten slightly on cookie sheet.

Bake at **350** for 10–12 minutes or until lightly browned.

# Chocolate Crackle Cookies

*Dramatic "crackles" and old-fashioned, chocolaty goodness!*

**MAKES 4 DOZEN**

½ cup oil
2 cups sugar
4 oz. baking chocolate, melted
2 teaspoons vanilla
4 eggs
2 cups flour
2–3 teaspoons baking powder
1 teaspoon salt
Powdered sugar for coating

Beat oil, sugar, chocolate and vanilla until blended. Beat in eggs. In a separate bowl, mix together flour, baking powder and salt. Gradually mix dry ingredients into sugar mixture. **Refrigerate dough 2 hours.**

Shape dough into 1" balls and roll in powdered sugar to coat generously and evenly. Place 2" apart on greased pan or baking mat.

Bake at **350** for 10–12 minutes.

# Lemon-Cornmeal Cookies

*A unique, not-too-sweet cookie brightened with a burst of lemon. My kids love these!*

MAKES 5-6 DOZEN

1 cup softened butter or shortening
1½ cups granulated sugar
2 eggs
1 teaspoon lemon juice
1 tablespoon fresh lemon zest
1 cup raisins
3 cups flour
1 teaspoon baking powder
1 teaspoon nutmeg
½ teaspoon salt
1 cup cornmeal

Cream together butter and sugar. Add eggs, one at a time, beating well after each. Mix in lemon juice, lemon zest, and raisins. In a separate bowl, mix together flour, baking powder, nutmeg, salt and cornmeal. Add flour mixture to sugar mixture and combine till well blended.

Place 1" balls on lightly greased cookie sheet or baking mat; flatten balls slightly with fingers.

Bake at **375** for 10–12 minutes.

# Old-Fashioned Raisin Bars

1 cup raisins
1 cup water
½ cup oil or melted butter
1 cup sugar
1 egg
1⅓ cup flour
¼ teaspoon salt
1 teaspoon baking soda
1 teaspoon cinnamon
1 teaspoon nutmeg
1 teaspoon allspice
½ teaspoon cloves
½ cup chopped nuts
Powdered sugar for dusting

Place raisins and water in small saucepan, bring to a boil. Boil until water is gone, remove from heat. Add in oil or butter and cool until lukewarm; transfer to mixing bowl. Add sugar and egg to raisins, blend. In separate bowl, mix flour, salt, baking soda, and spices. Add to raisin mixure. (Recommend stirring by hand to maintain integrity of raisins.) Stir in nuts.

Grease (or line with parchment) 9" x 13" baking dish, pour in batter.

Bake at **350** for 20 minutes, let cool.

Dust with powdered sugar and cut into bars.

# Coconut Refrigerator Cookies

MAKES 7–8 DOZEN

1 cup butter or margarine at room temperature
1 cup brown sugar
1 cup granulated sugar
2 eggs
1½ cups flour
1 teaspoon salt
1 teaspoon baking soda
3 cups rolled oats (oatmeal)
1½ cups coconut (shredded or flake)

Cream butter and sugars, beat in eggs. In a separate bowl, sift together flour, salt and baking soda. Add flour mixture, oats and coconut to butter mixture, mix well. (If dough seems wet, add more flour till it's the right consistency.)

Pack dough firmly into greased loaf pan, **refrigerate overnight**.

Cut dough in loaf pan into 1" slices. Work with one slice at a time and keep the remainder in the refrigerator until needed. Cut each slice into 12 equal squares; place squares on cookie sheet or baking mat.

Bake at **375** for 7-8 minutes.

**NOTE:** Dough can also be rolled into logs and refrigerated, then sliced to bake. Experiment with width of slice.

# Eve's Peanut Cookies

MAKES 6–7 DOZEN

1 cup butter or margarine at room temperature
1 cup brown sugar
1 egg
2 cups flour
1¼ teaspoons baking powder
1¼ teaspoons baking soda
1¼ cups oats (quick or regular)
½ cup cornflakes
1 cup Spanish peanuts

Cream butter and brown sugar. Beat in egg. In a separate bowl, combine flour, baking powder, and baking soda. Add to sugar mixture and blend well. Stir in oats, cornflakes and peanuts.

Drop dough by rounded teaspoon (or 1" balls) on greased cookie sheets or baking mat.

Bake at **350** for 12 minutes.

---

# COOKIE WISDOM

## Butter, margarine or shortening?

We found butter gave the best flavor to the recipes we tested, but that sometimes a shortening (like Crisco) made for a better texture, as noted in a few of the recipes. We didn't even try using margarine. And if a recipe in this book suggests using oleo (short for oleomargarine), you know it's truly vintage!

**Some background:** Shortening (e.g., Crisco) is 100% fat, containing no water (butter and margarine contain 15% water or more). That means no steam is created during baking, which effectively reduces gluten production, so shortening cookies tend to be softer and more tender. Also, shortening has a higher melting point than butter, resulting in taller cookies.

# Oatmeal Cookies

*My dad was a big fan of oatmeal cookies, and there was usually a batch in the cookie jar when I was growing up. Dad had one after dinner every night, so this recipe reminds me of him.*

MAKES 3-4 DOZEN, DEPENDING ON OPTIONAL ADDITIONS

1 cup butter at room temperature
1 cup granulated sugar
2 eggs
2 cups flour
2 cups oatmeal
1 teaspoon baking soda
½ teaspoon baking powder
¼ teaspoon salt
1 teaspoon cinnamon
¼ cup milk
*Optional additions:* Chocolate chips, raisins, nuts, etc.

Cream butter and sugar; add eggs and blend well. In a separate bowl, mix together flour, oatmeal, baking soda, baking powder, salt and cinnamon. Add dry ingredients to butter mixture, mix well, then add milk and mix again.

Drop by teaspoonfuls onto greased cookie sheet or baking mat, 1" apart.

Bake at **350** for 11–13 minutes or until lightly brown.

---

## COOKIE WISDOM

### Check on cookies 2-3 minutes before they should be done

If you like soft, slightly underdone cookies (like most humans do), be ready to take your cookies out of the oven 2-3 minutes before the recipe says they should be done.

Cookies burn easily, and oftentimes don't appear "done" on top when they're actually perfect. Thick or moist cookies are done when you can press lightly and leave a small imprint, while thin or crispy ones are done when they're firm to the touch and have slightly golden edges.

---

# Super-Easy Sugar Cookies

*I found this sugar cookie recipe in a magazine when my kids were young. It has served me well for holidays and birthdays—and made memories as my daughters and I decorated cookies. When they were little, I found a set of cookie cutters in the shape of numbers, so we made number cookies for their birthdays. It was so much fun telling the preschool teacher that I was bringing 3 cookies for a birthday, and she would ask, "Why are you only bring three cookies?" I would say, "Not three cookies, 3 cookies."*

2½ cups flour
2 teaspoons baking powder
1/4 teaspoon salt
1 cup butter or margarine at room temperature
1 cup granulated sugar
1 egg
1 teaspoon vanilla

Stir flour, baking powder and salt in a bowl; set aside. In a large bowl, with an electric mixer at medium speed, beat butter or margarine until smooth, gradually adding sugar until light and fluffy. Beat in egg and vanilla; add flour mixture and beat until well blended.

Roll out dough, cut it into shapes, and put them on a greased cookie sheet or baking mat.

Bake at **350** for 10 minutes or until bottoms of cookies are slightly brown. Remove to wire racks to cool.

Decorate.

## COOKIE WISDOM

### Store an apple wedge with your cookies

The moist apple wedge will let your chewy cookies steal some of its moisture, keeping them soft and tender for longer.

Also, make sure to wait to put away cookies once they've completely cooled — otherwise, condensation will build up and the cookies will turn soggy.

# Mom's Sugar Cookies

*These melt in your mouth! The powdered sugar added after baking gives them a wedding-tea-cake look.*

MAKES 6+ DOZEN

### Cream together:
1 cup butter at room temperature
1 cup vegetable oil
1 cup granulated sugar
1 cup powdered sugar

### Mix in:
2 eggs
1 teaspoon vanilla

### Sift, add, and mix well:
4 cups flour
1 teaspoon salt
1 teaspoon baking soda

> This will be a soft dough. Roll into 1" balls and place on cookie sheet.
> Bake at **375** for 10–14 minutes, till light brown.
> When completely cool, roll in powdered sugar.

---

## COOKIE WISDOM

### Dough Consistency: Too Wet

If your cookie dough seems too wet to maintain its shape when forming a ball or dropping from a spoon, add flour to the dough, a tablespoon at a time (or more if it's a large batch of dough), till you're happy with the consistency. Add a bit of sugar with each addition of flour to prevent floury taste.

It's not unusual when baking at high altitudes to add a little flour to cookie recipes. There's lots of technical advice about this on the internet; Google "high-altitude baking."

# Grandma Erie's Date Nut Cookies

*A delicious cookie with an elegant swirl. This recipe comes from my Grand-
mother Erie, Della May Ubel Albrecht.*

MAKES 5–6 DOZEN

## Dough:

2 cups brown sugar

1 cup butter or shortening

3 eggs

4 cups flour

½ teaspoon cinnamon

½ teaspoon salt

1 teaspoon baking soda

## Filling:

10–12 oz. package of dates, chopped

½ cup chopped pecans

½ cup granulated sugar

½ cup water

Cook filling ingredients together over low heat until syrupy. You may need
to add more water as it cooks down. Let it cool.

Mix dough until smooth and easy to roll; divide into three balls. One at a
time, roll each ball out to about 12"x18" and spread a third of the filling over
the dough. (It helps to roll out the dough on wax paper.) Beginning with the
wide side, roll the dough into a log about 2½" wide. Wrap the three logs tightly
in wax paper or plastic wrap and place on a cookie sheet in the freezer.

When the logs are frozen, cut into ¼" slices and place on lightly greased
cookie sheet or baking mat. Keep logs in freezer between batches; don't let
them thaw.

Bake at **350** for 7–10 minutes.

# d's Grandma's Molasses Ginger Cookies

*For a good five years, I was on the lookout for the world's best ginger cookie recipe. Then one Christmas, our daughter Megan's friend, "d" Williams, came over and brought with him some cookies his grandma had sent, and the quest came to an immediate end. Thanks to d's grandma Mary Scott for this recipe.*

MAKES 3–4 DOZEN

¾ cup butter at room temperature
1 cup granulated sugar, plus extra for coating
1 egg
¼ cup molasses
2 cups unbleached flour
2 teaspoons baking soda
1 teaspoon cinnamon
½ teaspoon salt
½ teaspoon ginger
½ teaspoon cloves

Cream butter, gradually add sugar, beating until light and fluffy. Add egg and molasses and mix well. In a separate bowl, combine flour, baking soda, cinnamon, salt, ginger and cloves. Mix well. Add about a quarter of the flour mixture to the butter mixture at a time, mixing well until smooth after each addition. **Chill dough 1 hour.**

Roll dough into 1" balls, then roll in sugar. Place balls on cookie sheets or baking mats.

Bake at **375** for about 10 minutes. When they turn out right, the tops will crack.

**NOTE:** Be careful with the size. When I rush and try to make them too large, they get flat and are not as good.

# Brown Sugar Drop Cookies

*This recipe is a favorite of ours, from John's grandmother, 'G.G.' It's traditional to bake them at Christmas.*

MAKES ABOUT 4 DOZEN

### Cream together:
½ cup butter at room temperature
1½ cups brown sugar

### Add:
2 eggs, beating after each

### Sift together, then add:
2½ cups flour
½ teaspoon baking powder
1 teaspoon baking soda
1 teaspoon salt

### Add:
1 cup sour cream
1 teaspoon vanilla
1 cup chopped nuts

Drop small spoonfuls on buttered cookie sheet (or baking mat). These spread quite a bit, so leave plenty of space between.

Bake at **350** for 10–12 minutes.

Wait till cookies are cool, then

### Frost with Buttercream Frosting:
1½ cups powdered sugar
3 tablespoons butter at room temperature
1 tablespoon plus 1 teaspoon milk
1 teaspoon vanilla

Combine all in small bowl, beat until smooth.

# Macklin's Raspberry Oatmeal Bars

*I don't bake too often anymore, but here is one of my faves! It came from our contractor in Durango, who was amazed that we remained married through building not one, but two houses about five years apart.*

MAKES 16–20 BARS

1¼ cups flour
1 cup brown sugar
1¼ cups quick oatmeal
½ teaspoon salt
¾ cup butter, melted
¾ cup raspberry jam

Mix together all but jam.

Pack half the oat mixture in greased 8" square pan, cover with jam, add rest of crumb mixture and pack firm, not hard.

Bake **325 to 350**, 40 to 50 minutes, until brown. Cool some, but take out of pan before completely cooled.

**NOTE:** Double the recipe for 9" x 13" baking dish.

---

## COOKIE WISDOM
### Using Vegetable Oil

If a cookie recipe calls for oil or vegetable oil, the best types to use are canola, sunflower, or grapeseed. We learned the hard way: make sure your oil hasn't been sitting around in your cupboard for a long time. Old vegetable oil makes your cookie taste like, well, vegetable oil!

Using vegetable oil in baked goods is known to give the moistest results. The reason is that vegetable oil remains liquid at room temperature, while butter turns solid.

**Substituting Oil for Butter:** Use half the amount of oil in cookie recipes that call for butter, but add liquid as needed. So if your recipe calls for 1 cup butter, substitute 1/2 cup oil and add liquid until the dough comes together and looks properly hydrated.

# Peanut Butter Balls

*Mom was working in surgical ICU in the early 1970s when she got this recipe from her best friend Marg. Mom said that while Dad was still here and helping with the rolling process, they would make 3 to 4 batches a year. After Dad was gone, she dropped back to just 2 or 3 batches. I know over the years we have all looked forward to getting that package in the mail at Christmas!*

MAKES ABOUT 250 BALLS

3 lbs. powdered sugar
2 lbs. peanut butter
1 lb. butter or margarine at room temperature
3 tablespoons vanilla
2 oz. edible paraffin wax, shaved
2 12-oz. packages chocolate chips

Combine powdered sugar, peanut butter, butter and vanilla.
Roll into 1" balls.
Melt chocolate and wax in double-boiler.
Dip balls into chocolate mixture and place on wax paper to dry.
Store in covered container(s) in refrigerator.

**NOTE:** Dipping is easier if you freeze the balls first. You can then insert a toothpick and use it as a handle for dipping and transferring balls to wax paper.

---

## COOKIE WISDOM

### Invest in insulated cookie sheets

If you bake a lot of cookies, insulated cookie sheets are worth investing in because they help cookies bake evenly and will not burn the bottoms. They're made with multiple layers of aluminum so that the air is insulated within the sheet, and not just whichever part of the oven is hottest.

# Canadian Rolled Oat Shortbread

*I got this recipe from a church cookbook a lady gave me when we visited Fairbanks, Alaska, in 1978. It is easy and delicious!*

1⅓ cups flour
1 cup shredded coconut
⅔ cup rolled oats (oatmeal)
1 cup butter at room temperature
⅔ cup brown sugar

Mix all ingredients to a crumbly mass and press into an 8" x 8" pan. Bake at **325** until light brown, 25–35 minutes.

# Cranberry-Nut Oatmeal Cookies

*Super-easy, super delicious oatmeal cookie!*

MAKES 4-5 DOZEN

4 cups oatmeal (regular oats)
1 cup chopped walnuts or pecans
1 cup dried cherries or cranberries or Craisins
1 cup flour
1 cup granulated sugar
1 cup brown sugar
2 eggs
2 teaspoons vanilla
1 teaspoon salt
1 teaspoon baking soda
1 cup butter or Crisco or do half of each

Place all ingredients except butter/Crisco in mixing bowl, stir well. Melt butter/Crisco and pour hot over oat mixture and mix thoroughly. **Allow mixture to set for 10 minutes to absorb oil.**

Dropped rolled balls on a greased cookie sheet or baking mat.

Bake at **350** till lightly brown, 11–13 minutes.

# Ginger Cookies

*These soft ginger cookies are a family favorite ... easy to make, freeze (if they get that far!) If I don't have the spices I need, I use pumkin pie spice.*

MAKES 3 DOZEN

3/4 cups shortening (can use butter, or half butter/half shortening)
1 cup granulated sugar
1 egg
4 tablespoons molasses
2 cups flour
1 teaspoon baking soda
1 teaspoon baking powder
1 teaspoon cinammon
1 teaspoon ginger
1/2 teaspoon cloves

Cream shortening and sugar. Add egg and molasses. Mix dry ingredients together and add to shortening mixture.

Roll in 1" balls, then roll in white sugar.

Put on ungreased baking sheet and bake at **350** for 10–11 minutes.

# Toffee Bars

*These are super easy and delicious. Fast to make when you don't feel like making individual cookies.*

1 cup butter at room temperature
1 cup brown sugar
1 egg yolk
1 teaspoon vanilla
2 cups sifted flour
1 cup semisweet chocolate chips
1 cup chopped walnuts or pecans

Thoroughly cream butter, brown sugar, egg yolk and vanilla. Add flour; mix well. Stir in chocolate chips and nuts.

Pat into ungreased 15" x 10" x 1" baking pan (jelly-roll pan).

Bake at **350** for 18-20 minutes. While warm, cut in bars.

# Loaded Oatmeal Cookies

*I love this recipe because you can use your choice of chips, fruit, and nuts for a different delicious result every time.*

MAKES 4-5 DOZEN

1 cup butter at room temperature
2 eggs, room temperature
¾ cup brown sugar
¾ cup granulated sugar
2 teaspoons vanilla
2 cups all-purpose flour
1 teaspoon baking powder
3/4 teaspoon baking soda
1 teaspoon salt
2 teaspoons cinnamon
1½ teaspoons milk
2½ cups oatmeal
12-oz. bag chocolate chips (or any other flavor chips)
1 cup raisins (or any other dried fruit, chopped if necessary)
1 cup chopped nuts (your choice of nuts)

Mix butter, eggs and sugars until light. Add vanilla and mix till combined. Sift together flour, baking powder, baking soda, salt and cinnamon; add to butter mixture and mix till combined. Add milk and mix till combined. Add oatmeal, chips, fruit and nuts, and stir by hand till combined.

Drop or roll dough onto ungreased cookie sheet. (Dough balls make for softer, thicker cookies; drop or flatten balls slightly for thinner, crunchier cookies.)

Bake at **375** for 10-13 minutes depending on size.

# Four Spice Cookie

*This is a "Dunker" passed down from Grandma Louise.*

MAKES 3 DOZEN

## Mix together into a creamy blend:
¾ cups of shortening: Crisco if you want crisp cookies, butter if you want softer cookies
1 cup granulated sugar
1 egg, unbeaten
¼ cup molasses

## Sift together in separate bowl:
2 cups all-purpose flour
2 teaspoons baking soda
¼ teaspoon salt
1 teaspoon cinnamon
¾ teaspoon cloves
¾ teaspoon ginger
½ teaspoon nutmeg

Mix dry ingredients into sugar/egg mixture just until blended.

Form into walnut-size balls and roll in baker's sugar (called Sugar in the Raw). Place 2" apart on a greased cookie sheet or baking mat.

Bake at **375** for 12 minutes. Cool on sheet for 5 minutes before transferring to rack. Store tightly covered or may be frozen.

**NOTE:** These will bake up nicer if the dough is refrigerated for a few hours prior to rolling into balls.

# High Altitude Chocolate Chip Cookies

*This is a large and somewhat costly recipe, but well worth it!*

MAKES 4½ DOZEN

**Sift together and set aside:**
2 cups minus 2 tablespoons cake flour
1⅔ cups bread flour
1¼ teaspoons baking soda
1 teaspoon baking powder
1½ teaspoons salt

**Cream in electric mixer, until very light (about 5 minutes):**
1¼ cups butter at room temperature
1 cup plus 2 tablespoons brown sugar
1 cup granulated sugar

Add 2 eggs, one at a time, mixing well after each addition. Stir in 1 tablespoon vanilla. On slow speed of mixer, stir in dry ingredients until just combined, and then add 1¼ pounds high-quality chocolate chips. Mix only until incorporated. Cover with plastic and **refrigerate 24 hours**.

When ready to bake, form generous scoops (golf-ball size) onto baking sheet covered with parchment paper or baking mat, about 2" apart.

Bake at **375** for 13 minutes until light golden. They may look underbaked but will firm up as they cool on sheet. Move to rack after set, about 10 minutes.

Dough will keep well in fridge for 72 hours.

**NOTE:** I don't usually bake them all at once. I bake a pan or two, then roll the rest into the cookie size I want, put them on a cookie sheet, freeze them for a few hours, then put the frozen, unbaked balls into a baggie and pop them back into the freezer for taking out a few at a time to bake.

# Snickerdoodles

*This is a recipe I found in a* Better Homes and Gardens Cookbook for Two *I was given as a wedding shower gift in 1962. I've made these Snickerdoodles many times over the years, passing the recipe down to my children as they grew up and had families of their own. Now my grown grandchildren are asking for the recipe.*

MAKES 2–2½ DOZEN, DEPENDING ON SIZE OF DOUGH BALL

½ cup butter at room temperature
¾ cup granulated sugar
1 egg
1⅓ cups flour
1 teaspoon cream of tartar
½ teaspoon baking soda
½ teaspoon salt

Mix butter, sugar and egg thoroughly. Sift remaining ingredients together and stir into first mixture.

Roll into small balls (about 1"). Roll each ball in a mixture of 1½ tablespoons sugar and 1½ teaspoons cinnamon. Place two inches apart on ungreased baking sheet.

Bake at **400** for 8–10 minutes until lightly browned but still soft. (They puff up at first, then flatten out.) Cool and store in covered container.

---

## COOKIE WISDOM
### Sifting vs. Not Sifting

Thanks to advances in the production of flour, it's no longer necessary to sift flour for most recipes. However, measuring flour accurately is critical to the success of your cookies. Always measure flour with nested metal or plastic cups.

If you are hand-mixing your cookies, it's a good idea to sift or whisk all the dry ingredients together to get rid of clumps (baking soda is especially likely to clump). Clumping isn't usually a problem if you're using an electric mixer.

# Half-Sugar Chocolate Chip Cookies

*This recipe calls for half the sugar of regular chocolate chip cookies, and substitutes half the flour with ground-up oatmeal. Amazingly yummy!*

MAKES 3-4 DOZEN

1 cup butter at room temperature
½ cup granulated sugar
½ cup brown sugar
2 eggs, beaten
1 teaspoon vanilla
1 teaspoon baking soda
1 teaspoon baking powder
1½ teaspoons salt
2 cups oatmeal
2 cups flour
1 cup chocolate chips
½ cup nuts, chopped

In a blender or food processor, grind the oatmeal till it resembles flour. Mix in separate bowl with the other dry ingredients.

Mix the first 5 ingredients together until well-blended, then add the dry ingredients. Stir in the chocolate chips and nuts.

Place walnut-size balls on ungreased cookie sheet or baking mat; flatten slightly.

Bake at **375** for 10–12 minutes.

## COOKIE WISDOM
### Flour your cookie cutters before use

If you're making sugar cookies or gingerbread cookies and using cookie cutter shapes, make sure to dip the cutters into flour before use. This way, the dough will loosen easily from the cutter when you place it on the cookie sheet.

You should put flour on your hands and the rolling pin for the same reason.

# Levain Bakery Chocolate Chip Crush Cookies

*This is a favorite recipe. It's a copycat from the Levain Bakery in New York City, one of my most favorite all-time treats. These cookies are HUGE, and some of the instructions are different than usual, but well worth it.*

MAKES 8 EXTRA-LARGE COOKIES

1 cup cold butter cut into small cubes
1 cup brown sugar
½ cup granulated sugar
2 eggs
1½ cup cake flour*
1½ cups all-purpose flour
1 teaspoon cornstarch
¾ teaspoon baking soda
¾ teaspoon salt
2 cups chocolate chips
2 cups walnuts, roughly chopped

In a large mixing bowl, cream together cold cubed butter, brown sugar, and granulated sugar for 4 minutes or until creamy. Add eggs, one at a time, mixing well after each one. Stir in flours, cornstarch, baking soda and salt; mix until just combined to avoid overmixing. Stir in chocolate chips and walnuts.

Separate dough into 8 large balls and place on light-colored cookie sheet. They are bigger than you think! You will fit 4 cookies on one large cookie sheet.

Bake at **410** for 9–12 minutes or until golden brown on the top. Let them rest for at least 10 minutes to set.

**NOTES:** Levain Bakery has stated they don't use vanilla in their cookies. If you would like to add vanilla extract, I would suggest adding 1 teaspoon when adding the eggs to the batter. (**Editors' Note:** We recommend adding vanilla.)

*Can substitute all-purpose flour for cake flour.

# Old Fashioned Molasses Cookies

*Pat Jurgens is the author of the novel "Falling Forward: A Woman's Journey West," in which Louisa opens a bakery in Golden, Colorado. This is a cookie authentic to the time and place of the novel (early 20th century); Louisa may very well have served these in her bakery.*

MAKES A LOT OF COOKIES!

1 heaping tablespoon baking soda
4–5 cups flour
1 pint Grandma's molasses
1 cup melted lard or shortening
2 eggs (no other wetting)
1 teaspoon cinnamon
1 tablespoon ginger
1 teaspoon salt

Combine all ingredients and let stand in icebox overnight.
Roll out ¼" to ½" thick. Cut in rounds or use gingerbread boy cookie cutter.
Bake at **350–375** for 10–12 minutes.

## COOKIE WISDOM

### Salted vs. Unsalted Butter

Bakers and chefs usually choose unsalted butter in their recipes because it's easier to manage the salt content in the dish. Most recipes that call for butter—especially baked goods and desserts—are created with unsalted butter. It is the standard in baking and is always implied unless otherwise specified.

But here's a general rule: Reduce or add 1/4 teaspoon of salt per 1/2 cup (1 stick) of butter. If you come across a recipe that calls for salted butter and all you have is unsalted butter, use unsalted butter and increase the salt in the recipe by 1/4 teaspoon for every 1/2 cup of butter.

# Wedding Balls

*Celebrated in German, Mexican and many other traditions.*

MAKES 30–33 BALLS

½ cup butter or margarine at room temperature
4 tablespoons powdered sugar, plus more for coating
½ teaspoon vanilla
¼ teaspoon salt
1 level cup unsifted flour
½ cup walnuts, chopped fine

Mix ingredients together. Form into walnut-size balls in palms of hands, place on ungreased cookie sheet or baking mat.

Bake at **325** for about 10–15 minutes. Done when bottom is brown.

Leave on cookie sheet to cool. When cold, roll balls in powdered sugar.

**NOTE:** Suggest doubling recipe—they melt in your mouth!—before storing in airtight container.

---

## COOKIE WISDOM

### Cookie Dough: To Chill or Not to Chill?

Chilling cookie dough before baking solidifies the fat in the cookies. As the cookies bake, the fat in the chilled cookie dough takes longer to melt than room-temperature fat. And the longer the fat remains solid, the less cookies spread. Chilled cookie dough produces a more evenly golden-brown cookie with a crisper edge and chewier center.

So even if the recipe doesn't say to chill the dough, consider putting it in the fridge for 30 minutes to 24 hours. That said, you should NOT chill the dough if you're looking for a thin or lacy cookie, where spreading is important.

To make forming the chilled cookie dough more manageable, pre-portion the dough by scooping balls of dough into individual cookies, place them on a sheet pan or in a Ziploc bag, chill, and then bake right away.

---

# Jumbo Raisin Cookies

*I received this recipe from my brother-in-law. Jumbo Raisin Cookies origi-nated with his mother, who worked in the school lunch program in the 1950s and '60s, at a time when everything was made from scratch and lard was a critical component of pie crust. She prepared family meals for her husband and nine children using the same homemade and time-consuming techniques.*

MAKES 4-5 DOZEN

1 cup water
2 cups raisins
1 cup butter or shortening
2 cups granulated sugar
2 eggs
1 teaspoon vanilla
4 cups flour
1 teaspoon baking soda
1 teaspoon salt
1½ teaspoons cinnamon
½ teaspoon nutmeg
¼ teaspoon allspice
1 cup nuts, chopped

Combine raisins and water in saucepan, boil 5 minutes. Cool to room tem-perature. Drain off excess liquid, if any.

Cream butter or shortening. Add sugar, eggs and vanilla, beat well. Sift to-gether flour, baking soda, salt and spices. Add to butter mixture and mix well. Stir in raisins and nuts.

Roll 1-tablespoon balls and place on ungreased cookie sheet or baking mat. Bake at **400** for 11–13 minutes.

# Chai-Spiced Shortbread Cookies

*These are my favorite cookies to make during the holidays. The mixture of sweet and spicy is just perfect with a cup of tea on a cold day. Everyone loves them!*

MAKES 2–3 DOZEN

1 cup butter at room temperature
½ cup granulated sugar
½ teaspoon salt
1 teaspoon vanilla
2 cups flour
1 tablespoon cinnamon
1¼ teaspoons ginger
1 teaspoon ground fennel seeds
½ teaspoon ground cardamom
Leaves from 1 English Breakfast tea bag
1 cup white chocolate chips

Beat butter, sugar, salt and vanilla in a large bowl with a mixer till smooth. In another bowl, stir together flour, cinnamon, ginger, fennel, cardamom and tea. Add to butter mixture and beat on low speed until blended. Stir in white chocolate chips.

Line two baking sheets with parchment paper. Set 1-tablespoon balls of dough 1" apart on sheets and flatten slightly with a floured glass.

Bake at **350** until cookies are light golden on undersides, about 15–18 minutes, switching pan positions halfway through baking (if using more than one pan at a time). Transfer to racks to cool.

# Chocolate Star Cookies

Makes 3-4 dozen

½ cup butter at room temperature
¼ cup peanut butter
½ cup brown sugar
½ cup granulated sugar
1 egg
1 teaspoon vanilla
1½ cups flour (can use gluten-free flour)
¾ teaspoon baking soda
½ teaspoon baking powder
3-4 dozen chocolate stars or Hershey's Kisses

Cream together butter, peanut butter and sugars. Mix in eggs and vanilla. In a separate bowl, mix flour, baking soda and baking powder together. Add to sugar mixture and blend well.

Shape dough into 1" balls and place on ungreased cookie sheet or baking mat. Press chocolate star or unwrapped Hershey's kiss into the center of each dough ball, flattening it slightly.

Bake at **350** for about 8 minutes.

## COOKIE WISDOM

### Baking with Oatmeal: Regular vs. Quick

**Regular oatmeal** (rolled oats) lends a slightly chewy texture to baked goods and the whole oats are clearly visible in the finished product, leading to more rustic looking cookies.

**Quick-cooking oats** are rolled oats that have been coarsely chopped. They have the exact same flavor as regular rolled oats, but a slightly finer texture. Cookies that are made with this type of oatmeal tend to look a little "prettier" because they don't have big oats floating around in them, and they give a baked good a very uniform texture. Quick-cooking oats can be made at home by pulsing regular oatmeal in the food processor a few times.

# Almond Cookies

*I usually double this recipe, because they are small cookies.*

MAKES ABOUT 2 DOZEN

½ cup butter at room temperature
¼ cup granulated sugar
¼ teaspoon almond extract
2 egg yolks, hard-boiled and sieved
1 cup flour
24 almonds, blanched

Cream butter. Mix in sugar, almond extract and egg yolks; blend in flour. Shape into 1" balls, place on ungreased cookie sheet or baking mat. Press one almond into each cookie.

Bake at **375** for 12 minutes.

**NOTE:** The dough will be crumbly, but will compress nicely when you're shaping it into balls.

**How to Blanch Almonds:** Bring water to a boil. Put almonds in water and boil for one minute, then take them out to cool. The almonds will slip out of their skin when you pinch them. Do not over-boil.

---

## COOKIE WISDOM

### Sprinkle coarse sea salt on chocolate chip cookies

Salty and sweet flavors always go really well together, but putting a sprinkling of sea salt on top of already delicious chocolate chip cookies before baking will make the chocolate seem even richer, and help the buttery, sugary dough taste even better.
    Try this once and you'll never go back.

# Pan-Fried Strawberry Cookies

*These always bring back memories of learning to bake miniature cookies with my cousin Marge in Boulder when I first moved to Colorado in 1968.*

MAKES 2–3 DOZEN

8 oz. dates, pitted and chopped
½ cup granulated sugar
1 egg, slightly beaten
½ cup shredded or flaked coconut
4 tablespoons butter
1 dash salt
1½ cups Rice Krispies
½ cup walnuts, chopped
1 teaspoon vanilla
Red sugar
Tube of green icing

In a skillet combine dates, sugar, egg, coconut, butter and salt. Cook and stir over medium heat until mixture bubbles and thickens, about 5 to 6 minutes. Remove from heat and add Rice Krispies, nuts and vanilla. **Cool for 10 minutes.**

Use 1 level tablespoon or less for each cookie. Moisten fingers and form into strawberry shape. While they are still warm, roll cookies in red sugar, then set on wax paper to cool. Top with green icing, using frilly edge to resemble leaves.

# Rocky Road Microwave Fudge

MAKES 16-24 PIECES, DEPENDING ON CUT SIZE

2 cups semisweet chocolate chips
1 (14 oz.) can of sweetened condensed milk
2 teaspoons vanilla extract
1½ cups chopped walnuts (optional)
1 cup miniature marshmallows

Grease 8" x 8" square pan.

Place the chocolate chips and milk in a medium-sized microwavable bowl. Microwave on high for 2 to 3 minutes, stirring occasionally, until smooth. Stir in the vanilla, then fold in the walnuts and marshmallows.

Spread evenly in prepared pan. Chill until set.

---

## COOKIE WISDOM

### 5 Reasons You Need a Silicone Baking Mat

**1. They can be reused over and over again.** A silicone baking mat can see more than 2,000 uses in the oven before it starts to show signs of age.

**2. They can do almost anything parchment can.** In addition to cookie work, baking mats can line baking sheets for freezing stuff (everything from fruit to cookie dough), roasting vegetables, and rolling out pie dough — just like parchment paper.

**3. They'll improve your cookies.** Got a terribly old baking sheet? A silicone baking mat creates a more even baking surface on even the worst baking sheets, resulting in cookies with more evenly browned bottoms — and fewer burnt cookies.

**4. No more worrying about whether to grease your cookie sheet.** You never have to grease your cookie sheet when using a silicone baking mat.

**5. They are easy to clean.** Silicone mats take literally seconds to clean. The amazing non-stick surface makes burned on pieces

---

# Chess Cake Squares

*This recipe is from my grandmother, Nanny Cole. She was the quintessential Southern cook. Everything she made was fabulous!*

1 box yellow cake mix
½ cup melted butter
4 eggs
8 oz. softened cream cheese
1 box or bag (16 oz.) powdered sugar

Lightly grease 9" x 13" baking dish.

Mix melted butter and 1 egg, beaten. Add yellow cake mix and mix till a stiff batter is formed.

Press batter into dish. Be sure to press batter ½" up all four sides to form a crust.

Mix cream cheese and 3 eggs till blended. Stir in powdered sugar, adding gradually. Mix filling batter well and pour into pressed crust.

Bake at **375** for 10 minutes; turn down to **325** for 30 minutes. Let cool completely before cutting.

# Cranberry Pecan Clusters

*So easy, and always a hit!*

MAKES 3 DOZEN

1½ cups pecans, chopped
1 cup dried cranberries
1 12-oz. bag Toll House Premium White Chocolate Morsels

Preheat oven to **350**. Place pecans on ungreased baking sheet and bake 7–10 minutes or until toasted. Stir after 4 minutes, and start checking at 7 minutes for doneness—they'll burn quickly!

In a microwave-safe bowl, microwave the white cholocate morsels on high at 30-second intervals, stirring periodically, until chocolate is melted. Add pecans and cranberries, stirring until coated with chocolate.

Drop by teaspoonfuls onto wax paper and let set. (Refrigerate for quick setting.) Store in airtight container.

# Mary's Toll House Cookies

*This is the Toll House recipe tweaked by my mom. There are a few changes for high altitude, and the sugar amounts have been lowered.*

MAKES 4 DOZEN

2¼ cups flour
½ teaspoon baking soda
½ teaspoon baking powder
1 teaspoon salt
1 cup shortening*
14 tablespoons brown sugar (¾ cup plus 2 tablespoons)
7 tablespoons granulated sugar (¼ cup plus 3 tablespoons)
2 eggs
1 tablespoon vanilla
1 12-oz. bag semisweet chocolate chips

Combine flour, baking soda, baking powder and salt in small bowl.

Beat butter, sugars and vanilla in large bowl until creamy. Add eggs, one at a time, beating well after each addition. Gradually beat in flour mixture. Stir in chocolate chips.

Drop by rounded tablespoon onto ungreased baking sheet or baking mat.

Bake at **375** for 9–11 minutes or until golden brown. Remove to wire racks to cool completely.

**\*NOTE:** I use butter-flavored Crisco for the best texture.

# Chocolate Drop Cookies

*These were my uncle's favorite.*

MAKES 3–5 DOZEN, DEPENDING ON SIZE OF SPOONFULS

½ cup butter at room temperature
1 cup brown sugar
1 egg
¾ cup buttermilk or sour milk*
1 teaspoon vanilla
3 oz. unsweetened (baker's) chocolate, melted
1¾ cups flour
1/2 teaspoon baking soda
1/2 teaspoon salt
1 cup chopped nuts

Cream together butter and brown sugar; beat in egg. Add buttermilk, vanilla and melted chocolate. Blend in flour, baking soda and salt. Mix well. Stir in nuts.

Drop by spoonfuls onto ungreased baking sheet.

Bake at **400** for 8–10 minutes, until no imprint remains when touched lightly with finger.

**\*To make sour milk:** Add 1 tablespoon vinegar or lemon juice to milk to make ¾ cup.

---

## COOKIE WISDOM

### Eggs-pert advice

Even though most of us store our eggs in the fridge, you're actually supposed to **use room temperature eggs when baking** since the whites and yolks combine easier and more evenly into the batter (leading to a better, airier cookie texture).

Getting eggs to room temperature is really easy—just place an egg in a bowl of warm tap water for 10-15 minutes.

# Soft Gingerbread Cookies
## (gluten-free or gluten-full)

*I first made this recipe after I discovered that my daughter has a strong gluten sensitivity. I made them for Thanksgiving gluten free and everyone loved them not knowing. I love them with a cup of Earl Grey tea.*

MAKES 2-3 DOZEN

2 cups flour **or** 2 cups Bob's Red Mill 1-to-1 Gluten Free Flour
½ teaspoon salt
2 teaspoons baking soda
½ teaspoon cinnamon
½ teaspoon cloves
½ teaspoon ginger
¾ cup shortening
1 cup granulated sugar plus about 1/4 cup for coating
1 egg
¼ cup molasses

In a mixing bowl, mix the flour, salt, baking soda, cinnamon, cloves, and ginger together. Set aside.

In a separate bowl, cream together the shortening, 1 cup granulated sugar, egg and molasses. Beat with an electric mixer for about 2 minutes. Add the dry mixture to the wet mixture and mix together until well combined.

Use a cookie scoop to scoop out tablespoon-sized balls and roll them into shape between your hands. Place the extra 1/4 cup of sugar in a small bowl and dip each cookie ball into the sugar, coating on all sides.

Place cookie dough balls on a cookie sheet and flatten slightly with the palm of your hand (or the bottom of a cup or glass).

Bake cookies at **350** for 10 minutes.

# Mudpies

*Quick and easy. No baking!*

MAKES 2–4 DOZEN, DEPENDING ON SIZE OF SPOON-DROPS

2 cups granulated sugar

1/2 cup cocoa (scant)

1/2 cup butter or margarine at room temperature

1/2 cup milk

1 teaspoon vanilla

1 teaspoon peanut butter

3 cups quick oatmeal

Mix cocoa and sugar together well. Bring sugar mixture, butter and milk to boil in pot; boil good for 1 minute. Remove from heat and add vanilla, peanut butter and oatmeal.

Drop by spoonfuls on wax paper or baking mats; let cool completely.

**NOTE:** Consider other additions, like nuts and coconut.

---

## COOKIE WISDOM

### Tips for Accurate Measuring

**DO** get yourself a set of proper measuring cups and spoons.

**DON'T** use liquid measuring cups for dry ingredients (though the other way around is okay).

**DO** read and follow directions carefully. "1 cup sifted all-purpose flour" and "1 cup all-purpose flour, sifted" are not the same the thing. You sift the flour before measuring it in the former and after in the latter, which leads to different amounts of flour.

**DON'T** use your measuring cup to scoop out flour. Spoon it into the cup and then level it off instead.

**DO** pack brown sugar into measuring cups and spoons. Packing is the standard way brown sugar is measured for all recipes.

**DON'T** pour vanilla and other liquids into the measuring spoon

---

# Orange Cookies

*It is my tradition to always bake these cookies for Christmas, and I have done so for probably 30 years. Recipe was shared by close friend in Conifer.*

MAKES 5–6 DOZEN

## Mix together:
¾ cup butter or Crisco
1½ cups brown sugar
2 eggs
1 teaspoon vanilla
1½ teaspoons grated orange rind (or more to taste)
½ teaspoon baking soda

## Sift together:
3 cups flour
1½ teaspoons baking powder
¼ teaspoon salt

Add the dry mixture to the wet mixture and mix together until well combined. Stir in ¾ cup broken nutmeats if desired.

## Make icing by stirring together:
2 cups powdered sugar
¼ cup orange juice
1½ teaspoons grated orange rind

Drop by small teaspoons on cookie sheet (lightly greased or with baking mat.) Bake at **375** until they begin to shrink; check every minute starting at 5 minutes. (Leave in a little longer if you like a crisp cookie.)

# Chocolate Nut Revels

*Easier than they look, and really, really tasty!*

5–6 DOZEN

1 cup chocolate chips
1 cup chopped pecans
1 cup butter at room temperature
⅔ cup sugar
¼ teaspoon salt
1 teaspoon vanilla
2 cups flour

Melt chocolate pieces over boiling water or in microwave. Stir in pecans and cool.

Cream butter, sugar, salt and vanilla. Blend in flour gradually. Add chocolate mixture to flour mixture and stir with fork, just enough to "revel" chocolate into white mixture—both colors should still be distinct.

Drop by teaspoon on ungreased cookie sheet or baking mat. Flatten to ¼" thickness with bottom of glass buttered or greased and dipped in sugar.

Bake at **350** for 12 minutes (13 minutes for crispy cookie).

# No-Bake Peanut Butter Balls

MAKES 6-7 DOZEN

2½ cups powdered sugar
2 cups crushed graham crackers (2 sleeves)
1 cup butter at room temperature
1 cup flaked coconut
¾ cup chopped dried apricots
¾ cup chunky peanut butter
1 teaspoon vanilla
⅓ cup granulated sugar

Blend all ingredients except granulated sugar.
Shape mixture into 1" balls, roll in granulated sugar.
Store covered in refrigerator.

# Chocolate Chocolate Chip

*This is from 'Mountain Mama's Cookie Blog.' These soft and chewy cookies disappear in quick order in our house. I gave my son a dozen one afternoon and he sent me a picture of the empty plate two hours later! They are the only cookies I make anymore.*

MAKES 5–6 DOZEN

2 cups flour
1¼ cups cocoa powder
1½ teaspoons baking soda
¼ teaspoon salt
1 cup butter at room temperature
1 cup granulated sugar
¾ cup brown sugar
2 eggs
1 tablespoon vanilla
1 cup white chocolate chips
1 cup semisweet chocolate chips
1 cup milk chocolate chips
Coarse sea salt (optional)

In medium bowl, combine the flour, cocoa, baking soda and salt. Set aside.

In a large bowl, cream the butter, brown sugar and granulated sugar until light and fluffy. Add eggs one at a time, beating well with each addition. Add vanilla and mix well. Gradually add in the flour/cocoa mixture and stir just until combined. Fold in chocolate chips.

Drop by rounded spoonfuls onto prepared cookie sheet (greased, parchment lined or baking mat). Sprinkle with a pinch of sea salt if desired.

Bake at **350** for 10–11 minutes until cookies are fluffy but still soft. Remove cookies from tray and place on cooling rack to cool completely.

# Yellow Cake Chocolate Chip Cookies

*Quick, cheap, but real good cookies!*

MAKES 3-4 DOZEN

1 box yellow cake mix
1 bag chocolate chips
1 cup oil
2 eggs, slightly beaten

> Mix cake mix and chocolate chips in large bowl. Mix in oil and eggs.
> Drop by teaspoons on greased cookie sheet or baking mat.
> Bake at **350** until edges are a little brown, 10–12 minutes.

**NOTE:** Also good with devil's food cake mix and coconut instead of yellow cake mix and chocolate chips.

# Spritz Cookies

*Crisp vanilla cookies made with a cookie press.*

MAKES 7–8 DOZEN

1 cup butter at room temperature
¾ cup granulated sugar
1 egg
1 teaspoon vanilla
2¼ cups flour
¼ teaspoon salt
Colored sugar (optional)

> Cream butter, then gradually add granulated sugar, creaming well. Beat in egg and vanilla. Mix flour with salt in separate bowl, and gradually mix into the sugar mixture.
> Press dough through cookie press in various shapes onto cold, ungreased cookie sheets. Sprinkle with colored sugar, if desired.
> Bake at **375** for 10 minutes, or until edges are lightly browned. Cool on racks.

# Cinnamon Sugar Cookies

*Easy cookies to make.*

MAKES 7–8 DOZEN

## Dough:
1 cup butter at room temperature
1 cup granulated sugar
1 cup powdered sugar
1 cup vegetable oil
2 eggs
1 teaspoon vanilla
4⅓ cups flour
1 teaspoon salt
1 teaspoon baking soda
1 teaspoon cream of tartar
1 teaspoon cinnamon

## Sugar Coating:
¼ cup granulated sugar
1 tablespoon cinnamon

Cream butter, sugars and oil. Beat in eggs and vanilla. In a separate bowl, combine flour, salt, baking soda, cream of tartar and cinnamon. Add dry mixture slowly until soft cookie dough is formed.

Roll dough into 1" balls, then roll in cinnamon/sugar mixture and flatten balls with a glass with decorative bottom (mine has multi-faceted bottom).

Bake at **375** for 10–12 minutes. After the first batch, add a little flour if cookie spreads too much.

# Greek Snow Balls

*These melt in your mouth. I've had this recipe for over 50 years. It came from a dear friend in the Greek community of Green River, Wyoming. Truly a family favorite at Christmas!*

MAKES LOTS!

1 pound sweet butter (unsalted, at room temperature)
¾ cup powdered sugar
½ teaspoon baking soda
½ tablespoon lemon juice
1 jigger whiskey
3–4½ cups flour
¾ cup walnuts or pecans, finely chopped (optional)

Beat butter until light and fluffy, then mix in powdered sugar and whiskey. Put baking soda in tablespoon and add lemon juice until bubbles form; add to butter mixture. Mix in 3 cups of flour, then keep adding flour gradually until soft cookie dough is formed.

Roll dough into small balls and place on cookie sheet or baking mat.

Bake at **375** until set and bottom is light brown, 10–12 minutes.

Once cookies are cool, roll in powdered sugar.

---

## COOKIE WISDOM

### Measuring flour

Too much flour can make some cookies rock-hard. When in doubt, error on the side of less flour; you can always add more if the first batch spreads too much while baking. Even better, use a scale if the recipe offers a weight equivalent. Spoon the flour into your measuring cup and sweep a spatula across the top to level it off. Do not use the measuring cup as a scoop or it will pack the flour and you will end up with more flour in the cup than intended.

# Almond Cookies
## (No gluten, no grain!)

*v..en in danger or in doubt, make good cookies, pass them out.*

MAKES 2+ DOZEN

2¼ cups almond flour
2 egg whites
1¼ cup powdered sugar
½ teaspoon lemon juice
¼ teaspoon baking powder
1 tablespoon almond extract
1 teaspoon vanilla extract

Whish almond flour, baking powder and powdered sugar. Beat egg whites and lemon juice until mixture stays in inverted bowl. Fold the dry ingredients into the egg whites. Add extracts and mix.

Form dough into 1" balls and **let sit one hour**.

Squash balls flattish. Bake at 360 for 17–20 minutes.

Dust cookies with powdered sugar if desired—messy and really sweet.

---

# COOKIE WISDOM

### Oh, nuts!

Smell and taste nuts before using. Oils in nuts can turn rancid quickly. Store any leftover nuts in the freezer for longest shelf life.

**Toasting nuts** draws the natural oils to the surface, intensifying the rich nutty essence, creating a deeper color, and making the nuts crunchier. Toasting your nuts prior to adding them to a recipe can improve the flavor and texture of any dish.

Line baking sheet with parchment paper. Spread the nuts out in a single layer. Bake for 5–10 minutes until the nuts darken in color a couple shades and the aroma of toasted nuts is strong in the kitchen. Check frequently; these will burn quickly!

# Rosemary Pine Nut Shortbread

*This recipe came from my dear friend Donna Connelly. Its flavors are a lit.*
*unusal and extremely delicious.*

¼ cup pine nuts
½ cup unsalted butter, melted
½ cup powdered sugar
1 tablespoon fresh rosemary (snipped from stems)
1 cup flour

Toast pine nuts for 5 minutes at 350. Watch closely; they burn easily.

Mix together melted butter, powdered sugar, rosemary and pine nuts. Stir in flour.

Spread in ungreased 8" square pan.

Bake at **350** for 20 minutes. Cool 2 minutes then cut in squares. Cool 10 more minutes before removing from pan.

---

# COOKIE WISDOM
## Healthy Substitutions

**Avocado for Butter:** This works best for recipes that are made with chocolate, such as brownies or cookies.

**Greek Yogurt for Cream:** Greek yogurt is an excellent replacement for heavy cream, sour cream, and cream cheese.

**Almond Flour for Regular Flour:** Works well in many types of non-yeast baking and can be mixed with regular flour or used alone.

**Applesauce for Sugar:** Replace the amount of sugar with applesauce, and decrease the amount of liquid in your recipe by 1/4 cup per cup of applesauce used.

**Flax Seed for Eggs:** Mix 1 tablespoon of ground flax seed with 2 1/2 tablespoons warm water to replace one egg.

**Cacao Nibs for Chocolate Chips:** These are crunchy, so can also be used to replace nuts.

*Google these substitutions for complete information.*

# Cranberry Cookies

*...ke to make these around the holidays, or whenever I can get fresh cranber-*
*...es. Very healthy!*

4 tablespoons butter or margarine at room temperature
1 cup brown sugar
½ cup applesauce
2 tablespoons molasses
2 tablespoons water
1 tablespoon vanilla
1 egg
2 cups oatmeal
1 cup flour
½ teaspoon baking powder
1 rounded teaspoon cinnamon
1 rounded teaspoon nutmeg
1 rounded cup whole cranberries, lightly chopped*
½ cup nuts, chopped
Grated orange rind to taste (up to ¼ cup)

Cream butter, sugar and applesauce. Blend in molasses, water, vanilla and egg. In separate bowl, mix together flour, oatmeal, cinnamon, nutmeg and baking powder. Add flour mixture to butter mixture and blend well. Stir in nuts, cranberries and orange rind.

Batter will be moist. Make small mounds on cookie sheet; they don't spread out much so you can get a lot on each sheet.

Bake at **375** for 10-12 minutes.

**\*NOTE:** The bigger the pieces of cranberry are, the more flavor per bite.

# Holiday Rum Balls

Makes about 3½ dozen

2½ cups vanilla wafers (appx. 75), crushed (but not too much)
1 cup ground pecans
1 cup powdered sugar (plus extra for coating)
2 tablespoons plus 2 teaspoons cocoa
¼ to ½ cup rum (or whiskey)
3 tablespoons light corn syrup
2 tablespoons water (or you can add more alcohol instead)

Mix all ingredients together, roll into 1" balls, roll in powdered sugar, put on wax paper to dry. Let dry before packaging.

**OPTIONS:** Used some crushed pretzels along with vanilla wafers. If the mixture is too sticky/wet, add more dry.

**TRY:** Inject maraschino cherries with rum to form center of balls.

---

# COOKIE WISDOM
## Making Your Cookies Gluten-Free

Substitute all-purpose gluten-free flour in place of all-purpose regular flour at a ratio of 1:1. Try **Bob's Red Mill** all-purpose gluten-free flour. If you are baking items such as cakes and/or breads, add 1 teaspoon of xanthan gum.

# Magic Cookie Bars

*siest and fastest cookie recipe on the planet! I always make this recipe for pecial occasions like Christmas and Easter, and I always make enough to give some away. It seems to be everybody's favorite.*

½ cup butter
1½ cups graham cracker crumbs (1 pkg./9 whole crackers)
1 can sweetened condensed milk
1 cup semisweet chocolate chips
1 cup butterscotch chips
1 cup chopped pecans
1 cup shredded coconut

Melt butter in 9" x 13" baking dish in oven.

Take dish out of oven and add graham cracker crumbs—spread evenly and pat down with back of spoon. Pour on the can of milk, covering the crumbs evenly. Add the chocolate and butterscotch chips. Add the nuts. Add the coconut and press down with back of spoon.

Bake at **350** for 25–30 minutes. Cool—refrigerate for easier cutting and removal.

---

## COOKIE WISDOM
### Read your cookie recipe carefully before starting

Be sure you have all the ingredients called for and that you understand the recipe clearly.

Remember: If something is worth doing, it is worth doing right! Cultivate the do-it-right attitude and habit. Baking demands accuracy and care. Unlike other kinds of cooking, such as soups or stews, you cannot improvise. Never carry on another activity while you are mixing a recipe. Distractions, no matter how small, lead to mistakes. Let the telephone ring!

# Canadian Cookies

*These were Dad's favorite!*

2 cups butter at room temperature
2 cups sifted flour
5 tablespoons powdered sugar plus extra for coating
1 cup pecans or walnuts, chopped
1 teaspoon water
1/2 teaspoon vanilla

Cream butter to whipped-cream consistency. Work in flour, powdered sugar and nuts. Add vanilla and water (doubling water if necessary to make mixture cling together).

Shape into marble-size balls; put in fridge to chill.

Bake at **400**, 10–12 minutes.

Roll in powdered sugar while hot.

# COOKIE WISDOM

## Cookies and salt

Salt is one of the major components that gives cookies their flavor, so it's important that you generously season the dough. Most quality cookie recipes will have at least a half teaspoon of salt in them — which might seem like a lot, but is necessary. If you're making up your own cookie recipe, don't be afraid to be a bit heavy handed. Both the dough and the chocolate is sweet, so it's important you use salt to balance them out.

**Note 1:** If you use salted butter in your dough, you can cut the amount of salt the recipe calls for in half.

**Note 2:** Kosher salt is a great salt for baking with. The small crystals dissolve easily and evenly season the dough.

# Mint Surprise Cookies

*hristmas tradition!*

1 cup butter at room temperature
1 cup granulated sugar
½ cup brown sugar
2 eggs
1 teaspoon water
1 teaspoon vanilla
3 cups flour
1 teaspoon baking soda
½ teaspoon salt
Chocolate-mint wafers (like Andes) or chocolate-mint chips

Cream butter and sugars till fluffy. Add eggs, water and vanilla, beat till thoroughly blended. In a separate bowl, mix flour, baking soda and salt. Add dry ingredients to butter mixture, mixing well.

Divide dough into four. Create logs, approximately 8" by 1½", and roll tightly in parchment paper, wax paper or plastic wrap, twisting the ends. **Refrigerate several hours or overnight.**

Cut logs in ¼" slices and place about 2" apart on cookie sheet or baking mat. Lightly push squares of chocolate-mint wafers (or several chocolate-mint chips) into each.

Bake at **375** for 9–10 minutes.

# The BEST Chocolate Chip Cookies

*My friend Julie DeLeeuw gave me this recipe. It truly is THE BEST!*

MAKES 6–7 DOZEN

## Beat until creamy:
1½ cups butter at room temperature
1½ cups brown sugar
1½ cups granulated sugar

## Add and mix till well-blended:
2 eggs
1 tablespoon vanilla

## In separate bowl, mix together:
3 cups flour
1 teaspoon salt
1 teaspoon baking soda

Add dry ingredients to wet mixture and mix till well-blended.

## Stir in:
2 cups regular oatmeal
3 heaping cups chocolate chips
3 heaping cups chopped roasted almonds (or other nuts)

Place golf ball-size balls of dough on ungreased cookie sheet (do not flatten). Bake at **350** for 12 minutes. (Cookies may not look done.) Let cool on sheet for awhile before moving to rack.

# Sugar Cookies

*these are so good dunked in coffee!*

MAKES 4–5 DOZEN

1 cup butter at room temperature
1 cup vegetable oil
1 cup granulated sugar
1 cup powdered sugar
2 eggs
1 teaspoon vanilla
4 cups flour
1 teaspoon baking soda
1 teaspoon cream of tartar

Cream butter, oil and sugars. Then cream in eggs and vanilla.

In a separate bowl, mix flour, baking soda, and cream of tartar. Add dry ingredients to creamed ingredients a cup at a time, blending well after each addition. **Chill in refrigerator at least 2 hours.**

Drop 1"–2" balls on cookie sheet, 2" apart (or use 1-tablespoon cookie scoop). For thinner cookies, flatten balls. Keep batter in refrigerator between batches.

Bake at **350** for 10–12 minutes or until edges are browned.

---

## COOKIE WISDOM

### What could be better than chocolate chips?

Chocolate chips are fine, but they're nothing special—and they're actually created so they don't fully melt, so you never get that perfectly gooey texture you're after. A simple upgrade is to use chopped chocolate or large chocolate discs available online and at speciialy stores. Both of these create large pockets of melted chocolate and take your cookies from good to great.

# Panocha Bars

*A version of chocolate chip cookies that can be prepared in about the sam̄
time that it takes to pre-heat the oven!*

¼ cup butter

1 cup brown sugar

1 large egg

1 teaspoon vanilla

1 cup flour

1 teaspoon baking powder

½ teaspoon salt

1 cup chocolate chips

¾ cup chopped, toasted walnuts or pecans

Melt the butter. While it is still hot, mix in the brown sugar, egg and vanilla until combined. In a separate bowl, whisk together the flour, baking powder and salt. Add flour mixture to butter mixture; mix until well combined. Stir in the chocolate chips and nuts.

Spread batter evenly into a greased 8" square pan.

Bake at **325** for 20–25 minutes, or until browned on top and toothpick in the center comes out clean. Let cool completely, then cut into bars.

---

## COOKIE WISDOM

### Don't Put Dough on a Hot Cookie Sheet

Make sure to let your sheet trays completely cool before baking another batch on them. If you can't fit all of your cookies on your sheet tray and need to bake them in multiple batches, make sure to let your sheet tray completely cool before scooping your next batch of dough onto it. If you were to scoop them onto a tray that's still hot, the bottoms may burn and your cookies may spread too quickly.

# Brown Sugar Thumbprint Jam Cookies

*beautiful and deliciously tender cookie from my mother-in-law's kitchen ..at was always a part of our Christmas.*

1 cup butter at room temperature
½ cup brown sugar
1 large egg yolk
1 teaspoon vanilla
¼ teaspoon salt
2 cups flour
1 egg white, beaten, for rolling
Chopped nuts for rolling
Raspberry jam (or jam of your choice)

In an electric mixer, cream together the butter and brown sugar. Then add the egg yolk, vanilla and salt, and combine well. Mix in flour gradually until a dough forms.

With a fork, beat the egg white until just foamy. Form dough into 1-table-spoon balls and roll in the beaten egg white to cover. Then roll in the nuts and put on a cookie sheet. Make a depression in the dough with your thumb and spoon a little jam just to fill the depression (don't overfill).

Bake at **350** about 16–18 minutes, until slightly brown.

**COOK'S WARNING:** These can be very addicting, but they are oh, so yummy!

# Wendy's Biscotti

*Quick to whip up ... everyone's favorite ... ships beautifully! This recipe* ι
*Wendy Baker was published in the Feb. 1995 issue of* Gourmet *magazine.*

MAKES ABOUT 24 BISCOTTI

½ cup unsalted butter, at room temperature
¾ cup sugar
1 tablespoon freshly grated orange zest
½ teaspoon vanilla
2 large eggs
2 cups flour
1½ teaspoons baking powder
¼ teaspoon salt
2 oz. white chocolate, chopped coarse (about 1/2 cup)
½ cup dried currants
1¼ cup natural shelled pistacios

Preheat oven to 325 and lightly grease a large baking sheet.

In a bowl with an electric mixer, beat together butter, sugar, orange zest and vanilla until light and fluffy. Add eggs, one at a time, beating well after each addition.

In a separate bowl, sift together flour, baking powder and salt, and gradually beat into butter mixture, beating until combined well. Stir in remaining ingredients. **Chill dough 30 minutes, or until it no longer feels sticky.**

Turn dough out on a lightly floured surface and halve. Form each piece into a flattish log about 12" long by 3" wide. Arrange logs at least 3" apart on baking sheet and bake in middle of oven until golden, about 30 minutes. Cool logs on baking sheet on a rack 5 minutes.

On a cutting board, cut logs crosswise on a diagonal into 1"-thick slices and arrange biscotti, cut sides down, on baking sheet. Bake biscotti in middle of oven 15 minutes, or until golden. Transfer biscotti to racks and cool completely. Store in an airtight container at room temperature.

**NOTE:** You can use mix-ins of your choice—instead of white chocolate, for example, you can use milk, semisweet or bittersweet chocolate chips; instead of dried currants, use chopped dried cherries or chopped dried cranberries; and instead of pistachios use chopped toasted pecans or walnuts.

# Lace Cookies

*ce cookies were always for a fancy occasion, like a tea party or company.*
*veryone would comment how unusual and delicious they were.*

MAKES 4–5 DOZEN

½ cup butter or margarine at room temperature
1½ cups quick-cooking oats
¾ cup granulated sugar
1 tablespoon flour
1 teaspoon baking powder
½ teaspoon salt
1 egg
1 teaspoon vanilla
½ cup nuts, chopped

Melt butter and pour over oats in large bowl. Mix with fork. In separate bowl, mix together sugar, flour, baking powder, and salt. Add flour mixture to oats. Add egg and vanilla, mix well. Stir in nuts. **Refrigerate overnight.**

Roll dough into marble-size balls (appx. 1 teaspoon) and place on foil-lined cookie sheet.

Bake at **350** for 8–10 minutes. These will spread! Move foil with cookies to cooling rack; cool before storing.

---

## COOKIE WISDOM

### Don't Over-Mix Your Dough

Keep your mixer on low unless you need to cream or whip something. Stop mixing when there's just a little bit of flour still visible — if you're adding things like nuts or chocolate chips it will mix in when you stir in the final ingredients, and if not, it will mix in as you scoop out the dough. Not over-mixing your dough can make the difference between ho-hum and WOW!

# Peanut Butter Cookies

*These were my favorite and my Mom, a home economics teacher, would a*
*ways mail me a box when I was away at a camp or in college and even afte*
*I got married. She would pack them in real popped corn so they wouldn't*
*crumble—and I always ate the popcorn as a snack!*

MAKES ABOUT 6 DOZEN

1 cup butter or shortening
1 cup granulated sugar
1 cup brown sugar
2 eggs
1 teaspoon vanilla
1 cup peanut butter
2½ cups flour
1 teaspoon baking soda
1 teaspoon salt
1 teaspoon baking powder

Cream together shortening, sugars, eggs and vanilla till light and fluffy.
Stir in peanut butter. Sift together flour, baking soda, salt and baking powder,
stir into creamed mixture.

Form in small balls; place about 2" apart on ungreased cookie sheet. Press
with back of fork to make crisscross pattern.

Bake at **375** about 10 minutes. Cool slightly and remove from pan.

# Monster Cookies

*family favorite! Makes a LOT!*

MAKES 10+ DOZEN

6 eggs
1 cup butter at room temperature
2½ cups brown sugar
2 cups granulated sugar
3 cups peanut butter
½ teaspoon vanilla
1½ teaspoons honey
4 teaspoons baking soda
1 cup flour
9 cups oatmeal
½ lb. M&M's
1 cup milk chocolate chips

Combine eggs, butter, brown sugar, granulated sugar and peanut butter. Add vanilla, honey and baking soda. Mix well. Stir in flour, oatmeal, M&M's and chocolate chips until well blended.

Line cookie sheets with parchment paper or baking mats. Place 2-tablespoon scoops of dough on cookie sheets, at least 2" apart.

Bake at **350** for 10–12 minutes until tops look set. Do not over-bake if you want chewy cookies; leave them on the cookie sheet for a while before moving to racks, and they will continue to harden as they cool.

# Butterscotch Toffee Cookies

*For people who want to make an easy cookie. I made these for one of t.*
*Camp Comfort sessions.*

MAKES 3–4 DOZEN

2 large eggs, room temperature
½ cup canola oil
1 package butter pecan cake mix (regular size)
1 package (10 to 11 oz.) butterscotch morsels
1 package (8 oz.) milk chocolate English toffee bits

In a large bowl, beat eggs and oil until blended. Gradually add cake mix and mix well. Fold in chips and toffee bits.

Drop by tablespoonfuls 2" apart onto greased cookie sheet or baking mat.

Bake at **350** until golden brown, about 10–12 minutes. Cool 1 minute before removing to wire racks.

---

# COOKIE WISDOM

### First steps: Creaming butter & sugar, beating the eggs

**Creaming** is the process of beating softened butter and sugar together until light and fluffy. This stage is essential to the quality of dough you produce.

When you beat butter and sugar together in a cookie recipe, you're not just combining ingredients. You're aerating the dough, and creating tiny pockets of air that puff up once the cookies hit the oven. When not done properly, your cookies will end up dense and flat, and no one wants that!

**Beating in the eggs** takes more time than you think. Add the eggs gradually, beating really well between each addition. The eggs add volume, giving depth to your cookies.

# Chocolate Chocolate Chip Cookies

*r a healthier cookie, I use half sugar/half Splenda, half butter/half apple-*
*auce, half white flour/half whole wheat flour, and 1 cup chocolate chips.*

MAKES ABOUT 4 DOZEN

1 cup butter at room temperature
1½ cups granulated sugar
2 eggs
2 teaspoons vanilla
2 cups flour
⅔ cup cocoa powder
¾ teaspoon baking soda
¼ teaspoon salt
2 cups semisweet chocolate chips
½ cup chopped walnuts or pecans (optional)

In large bowl, beat butter, sugar, eggs and vanilla until light and fluffy. In a separate bowl, combine flour, cocoa, baking soda and salt; stir into the butter mixture until well blended. Mix in the chocolate chips and nuts.

Drop by rounded teaspoonfuls onto ungreased cookie sheet or baking mat.

Bake at **350** for 11–12 minutes. Cool slightly on the cookie sheets before transferring to wire racks to cool completely.

## COOKIE WISDOM

### A sweet rolling hack

Use powdered sugar—instead of flour—when rolling out dough. The sugar melts into the dough while baking and doesn't leave a white dusting on your treats.

# Salted Chocolate Butter Pecan Cookies

*These shortbread cookies are nutty, sweet and salty!*

MAKES 2 DOZEN

2 sticks (1 cup) salted butter, at room temperature
2 teaspoons vanilla
½ cup dark brown sugar
1¾ cups all-purpose flour (plus ¼ more, as needed)
¾ cup pecans, very finely chopped
1 large egg, beaten
1 cup coarse turbinado sugar
1½ cups semisweet or milk chocolate, melted
Flaky sea salt

Add 1 stick butter to a small aucepan set over medium heat, cooking until the butter begins to brown, about 3–4 minutes. Remove from heat and transfer to a heat-proof bowl. Place in the freezer to chill 10–15 minutes, but no longer.

In a large mixing bowl, beat together the remaining stick of butter, the cooled browned butter, brown sugar and vanilla until creamy. Add the flour and mix until fully combined. If the dough is still too sticky to form a ball, add additional ¼ cup of flour. Stir in the pecans.

Place the dough on a large piece of wax paper or plastic wrap. Using your hands, shape it into a log about 12" long and about 2" in diameter. Wrap the dough up in the wax paper and **place the dough in the fridge for 2 hours or up to 5 days.**

Preheat oven to **350**. Line a baking sheet with parchment paper.

Unwrap the dough and place it on a cutting board. Brush the dough with the beaten egg and roll in the coarse turbinado sugar to coat. Using a sharp chef's knife, cut the log into ½" slices. (It is important to cut in a quick forward motion. Do not move the knife back and forth. If the dough cracks, just push the dough rounds back together. Promise it will be okay!) Arrange the slices on the prepared baking sheet. Bake the cookies for 12–14 minutes, until the edges are golden brown. Let the cookies cool on the baking sheet.

Drizzle the chocolate over each cookie and sprinkle with sea salt. To harden the chocolate, place the tray of cookies in the fridge for 10 minutes. Store cookies in an airtight container for up to 4 days at room temperature.

# Christmas Jolly Hollies

*e always made these on December 23rd, the night our kids—and now our grandkids—sleep under the Christmas tree.*

MAKES 3 DOZEN

5 cups corn flakes
½ cup butter
40 large marshmallows
1 small bottle green food coloring (use just as much as you want for the color)
1 teaspoon vanilla
Red Hots

Melt butter; add marshmallows and stir until they melt. Add food coloring and vanilla; stir till blended. Add cornflakes and stir until coated.

Butter fingers and use a spoon to "plop" cookies onto wax paper. Place two red hots on each (while hot). Let cool.

**NOTE:** Using different food colorings, this mixture can be molded into just about any shape—hearts for Valentine's Day, bunnies for Easter, wreaths for Christmas, etc.

---

## COOKIE WISDOM

### Is Pure Vanilla Worth the Price?

**Pure vanilla** adds a distinctive warm, round, sweet note to anything it is added to. Imitation extract adds a hint of this, but the real thing instantly brings your baked goods and desserts to a much higher level.

**Imitation vanilla** is made from artificial flavorings, which isn't surprising. People with discerning palates usually find that imitation vanilla products have a harsh quality with a slightly bitter aftertaste.

**Vanilla flavoring** is usually a combination of imitation vanilla and pure vanilla extract. It's cheap, but that may be the best that can be said for it.

# Ginger Cookies

*This is Mike's grandmother's (Gladys Tindall) recipe.*

MAKES 5–6 DOZEN

¾ cups unsalted butter at room temperature
1½ cups granulated sugar plus extra for coating
2 large eggs
4 tablespoons honey
1¾ teaspoons baking soda
Pinch of salt
2½ cups flour
1 teaspoon cinnamon
1 teaspoon ginger
½ teaspoon cloves

Mix all ingredients in order and **chill 2 hours or overnight**.

Roll in a 1" ball, then roll in additional white sugar. Place on parchment-lined baking sheets (or baking mats). Do not flatten.

Bake at **350** for 8–10 minutes. The cookies flatten out as they are removed from the cookie sheet. Cool on a rack.

---

## COOKIE WISDOM
### Use a cooling rack

Letting your cookies cool directly on the hot pans will continue to cook them, which can lead to over-browning on the bottoms. In addition, because the steam can't escape as well when the cookies are sitting on the pan, they can get a bit soggy. As soon as they're cool enough to move (no more than 2 to 3 minutes), transfer them with a spatula to a cooling rack with at least 1/2-inch of clearance underneath to ensure proper airflow. The best racks for cookies are formed from a tight wire grid (rather than the wide bars of a roasting rack).

Made in the USA
Columbia, SC
05 December 2021

50265144R00039